P9-CCX-726

Holiday ★ Histories

Columbus Day

Mir Tamim Ansary

Heinemann Library
Chicago, Illinois

© 1999 Reed Educational & Professional Publishing
Published by Heinemann Library,
an imprint of Reed Educational & Professional Publishing,
100 North LaSalle Street, Suite 1010
Chicago, IL 60602
Customer Service 888-454-2279
Visit our website at www.heinemannlibrary.com

Printed and bound in Hong Kong

03 02 01 00
10 9 8 7 6 5 4 3 2

Library of Congress Cataloging-in-Publication Data

Ansary, Mir Tamim, 1954-
    Columbus Day / Mir Tamim Ansary.
        p.   cm. — (Holiday histories)
    Includes bibliographical references and index.
    Summary: Introduces Columbus Day, explaining the historical events behind it, how it became a holiday, and how it is observed.
    ISBN 1-57572-702-1 (lib. bdg.)
    1. Columbus Day—Juvenile literature. 2. Columbus, Christopher—Juvenile literature. 3. America—Discovery and exploration—Spanish—Juvenile literature. [1. Columbus Day. 2. Columbus, Christopher. 3. Eorers. 4. America—Discovery and exploration—Spanish. 5. Holidays.] I. Title. II. Series: Ansary, Mir Tamim. Holiday histories.
E120.A67   1998
394.264—dc21   98-13721
                                                          CIP
                                                          AC

Acknowledgments
The publisher would like to thank the following for permission to reproduce photographs:

Cover: The Granger Collection
Map Illustrator: Yoshi Miyake

Photo Edit/Spencer Grant, p. 5; The Granger Collection, pp. 6, 10, 12, 15, 16, 17, 19, 21, 22, 23; Stock Boston/Bob Daemmrich, pp. 7, 26; Culver Pictures, Inc., p. 9; Tony Stone/Richard A. Cooke III, p. 11; Super Stock, pp. 14, 18, 24; Photo Edit/Anna E. Zuckerman, p. 20; Photo Edit/David Young Wolff, p. 25; Photo Edit/John Neubauer, p.27; NASA, p. 29.

Every effort has been made to contact copyright holders of any material reproduced in this book. Any omissions will be rectified in subsequent printings if notice is given to the publisher.

Some words are shown in bold, **like this**. You can find out what they mean by looking in the glossary.

Contents

A Noisy Parade

There is a noisy parade downtown today. It happens every year on October 12. Many people in this parade are Italian American, for this is Columbus Day.

Many cities have a Columbus Day Parade. They **honor** an explorer named Christopher Columbus. He was born in Genoa, Italy, in 1451. He died in 1506.

Why Columbus is Famous

Columbus is famous for one reason. He sailed to America in 1492. Many people say that Columbus **discovered** America.

These **Native Americans** are **protesting** the idea that Columbus discovered America.

This is not true. Columbus did not get here first. America was already full of people when he came.

★

The First Americans

The first Americans came from Asia long, long ago. These people walked to America. A strip of land connected the two **continents** back then.

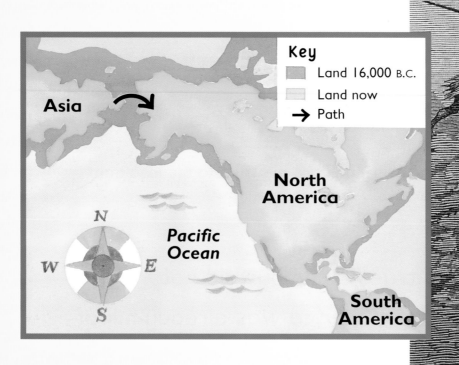

Key
- Land 16,000 B.C.
- Land now
- → Path

Asia

North America

Pacific Ocean

N
W E
S

South America

Over time, water covered up the strip of land. The Americas were then cut off from the rest of the world.

Two Separate Worlds

Thousands of years passed. People in Europe, Asia, and Africa built great cities. The people in those cities did not know about the Americas.

Great cities were built in the Americas, too.
The people in these cities knew about each
other. But they knew nothing of the other
continents.

★

Europeans Explore

About five hundred years ago, some **Europeans** became great sailors. They wanted to sail to the islands east of India. Those lands were called the **Indies**.

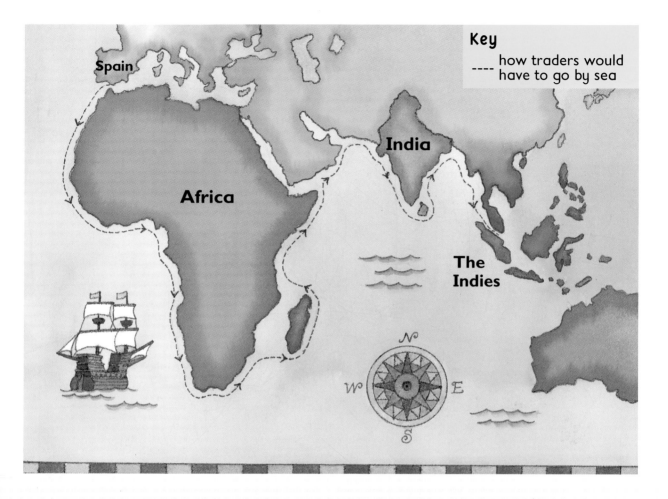

Key
---- how traders would have to go by sea

Spain

India

Africa

The Indies

Traders had reached the Indies by land. From there, they had brought back spices, silk, and other rich **goods**. But no one had reached the Indies by sea. The trip was too long.

A Crazy Idea

Christopher Columbus knew the world was round. He had an idea. Why not get to the **Indies** by sailing west? It might be quicker, thought Columbus.

Most people called Columbus crazy. They
said the ocean was too big to cross. They
said sea monsters would get him.

★
15

A Queen Listens

But one person listened. She was Isabella, queen of Spain. She wanted the **goods** of the **Indies**. She hoped Columbus would find a shortcut to those islands. She decided to help him.

Isabella gave Columbus three ships. They were called the *Nina*, the *Pinta*, and the *Santa Maria*. She gave him 90 sailors. Columbus headed out to sea.

Crossing the Ocean

He sailed for weeks. His sailors got scared.
They begged Columbus to turn back.
Columbus said no. The sailors were about
to kill him when . . .

. . . they spotted an island! Columbus thought it was part of the **Indies**. So he called the people who lived there "Indians."

A New World

Columbus had landed in the Bahamas, hundreds of miles from what is now Florida. West of these islands lay North and South America. **Europeans** had never seen these **continents**.

After Columbus, many Europeans sailed to the "New World." **Priests** came to spread the Christian religion. Soldiers came to find gold.

Europeans Take Over

Europeans spread all over the Americas. They cut down forests and planted farms. They built new cities. They tried out new ways of life.

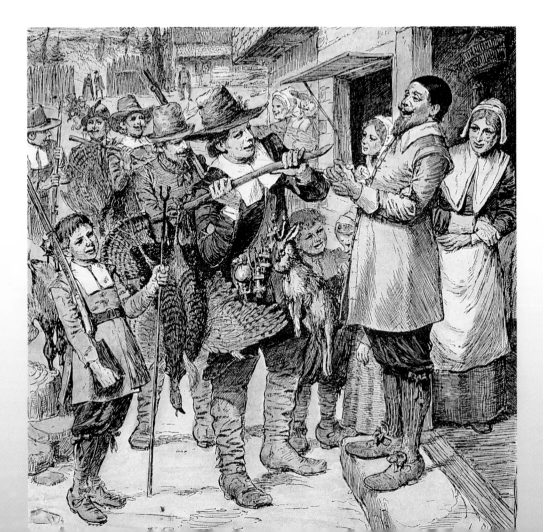

The Europeans fought with the **Native Americans**. They destroyed many Native American cities. And European **germs** killed many Native Americans, too.

The Native Americans

But **Europeans** also learned from the **Native Americans**. They learned about new foods, such as potatoes, corn, squash, peppers, and turkey.

★

Some Europeans mixed with the Native Americans. Out of the mixture came new people. Twenty-three new nations rose in the Americas. One of them is our country.

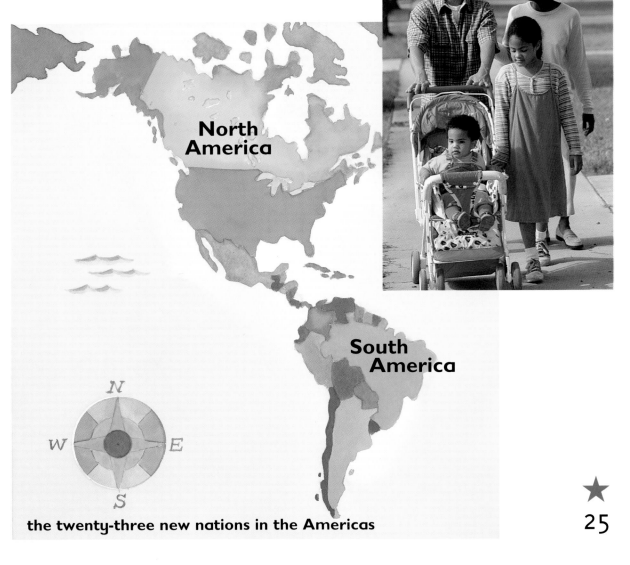

the twenty-three new nations in the Americas

Celebrating Columbus Day

Columbus Day was first celebrated in Colorado in 1907. Today it is a national holiday.

Replicas of Columbus's ships in Corpus Christi, Texas

Columbus Day is celebrated in other
countries, too. In Costa Rica, for example,
it is called Culture Day.

Into the Unknown

Today, the whole world has been mapped. But there is still much to explore. Look up at the night sky. You are looking into the **unknown**.

This picture was taken on Mars by the Mars Pathfinder spacecarft in 1997.

Columbus sailed into the unknown without fear. And we still need his spirit. We are still exploring. And that is why we celebrate Columbus Day.

★

Important Dates

Columbus Day

30,000 B.C.–10,000 B.C.	First Americans come from Asia
around 500	Teotihuacan is at its greatest
around 550	Constantinople is at its greatest
around 1400	**Europeans** begin to explore the world
1451	Christopher Columbus is born
1492	Columbus sails to America
1506	Columbus dies
1519	Cortez destroys the Aztec capital in Mexico
1532	Pizarro destroys the Inca capital in Peru
1907	Colorado celebrates the first Columbus Day

Glossary

continents large land areas of the earth

discovered to find something that no one knew about

Europeans people from Europe

germs tiny life forms that make people ill

goods things people use

honor to show respect for something or someone

Indies Indonesia and other islands east of India

Native Americans another name for American Indians

Priests leaders in a Christian church

protesting showing that you disagree with something

replicas copies of something

unknown something that we know nothing about

More Books to Read

DeRubertis, Barbara. *Columbus Day: Let's Meet Christopher Columbus.*
New York: Kane Press, 1996.

Liestman, Vic. *Columbus Day.* Minneapolis, Minn:
Lerner Publishing Group, 1991.

Moncure, Jane. *Our Columbus Day Book.* Chanhassen, Minn:
Child's World, 1986.

Index